HANDS-ON HISTORY

CELTS

DRESS, EAT, WRITE, AND PLAY JUST LIKE THE CELTS

JOE FULLMAN

QEB Publishing

Published in the United States by
QEB Publishing, Inc.
3 Wrigley, Suite A
Irvine, CA 92618

www.qeb-publishing.com

Library of Congress Cataloging-in-Publication Data

Fullman, Joe.
  Celts : dress, eat, write, and play just like the Celts /
Joe Fullman.
    p. cm. -- (QEB hands-on history)
  Includes index.
  ISBN 978-1-59566-247-7 (hardcover)
  1. Celts--Juvenile literature. 2. Celts--Social life and
customs--Juvenile literature. 3. Civilization, Celtic--
Juvenile literature. I. Title.
  D70.F85 2010
  936.4--dc22
                                          2009001116

Author Joe Fullman
Consultant John Malam
Editor Ben Hubbard
Designer Lisa Peacock
Project Maker Veronica Lenz

Publisher Steve Evans
Creative Director Zeta Davies
Managing Editor Amanda Askew

Printed and bound in China

Picture credits
(t=top, b=bottom, l=left, r=right, c=center, fc=front cover)
Alamy Images 4bl David Lyons, 7tl Nearby, 8b Mary Evans Picture Library, 10t North Wind Picture Archives, 10bl Detail Heritage , 11t The London Art Archive/ Visual Arts Library (London), 16t Orkneypics, 16bl John Warburton-Lee Photography, 22t North Wind Picture Archives, 22b Lebrecht Music and Arts Photo Library, 26t Imagebroker/Christian Handl
Bridgeman Art Library 12b Private Collection/Look and Learn
Corbis 12t Werner Forman, 12c Werner Forman, 14bl Chris Warren/Loop Images/Loop Images, 18b Werner Forman, 20b Bettmann, 24b Bettmann, 26b Bettmann, 28t, Robert Holmes
Dreamstime 8t Frederik Sadones
Getty Images 6t Hulton Archive/MPI/Stringer, 6b Dorling Kindersley/Max Alexander, 14t National Geographic/ Ira Block, 20c The Bridgeman Art Library
Photolibrary 15t John Warburton-Lee Photography
Rex Features 19tl, 20t Peter Brooker
Shutterstock 4t Mark Beckwith, 24t Zbynek Burival
Simon Pask 4cr, 4br, 5cl, 5cr, 5bl, 5br, 7tc, 7tr, 7cl, 7cr, 7bl, 7br, 9tl, 9tr, 9cl, 9cr, 9bl, 9br, 10cr, 10br, 11cl, 11cr, 11bl, 11br, 13tl, 13tr, 13cl, 13cr, 13bl, 13br, 14cr, 14bc, 14br, 15cl, 15cr, 15bl, 15br, 17tr, 17tl, 17cl, 17cr, 17bl, 17br, 19tr, 19cl, 19cr, 19bl, 19br, 21tl, 21tr, 21cl, 21cr, 21bl, 21br, 27tl, 27tr, 27cl, 27cr, 27bl, 27br, 23tl, 23tr, 23cl, 23cr, 23bl, 23br, 25tl, 25 tr, 25cl, 25cr, 25bl, 25br, 28bl, 28cr, 28br, 29tl, 29tr, 29bl, 29br
Topham Picturepoint 5t The Granger Collection, 16br, 18t The Granger Collection

With thanks to Galloway Glass for the use of the Celtic symbols, page 25

TAKE CARE WHEN USING SCISSORS

Words in **bold** are explained in the glossary on page 30.

CONTENTS

WHO WERE THE CELTS?

The Celts were an ancient people who first appeared in Europe about 2,500 years ago. The Celts settled across much of the continent and for centuries were the dominant people in Europe. As time went on, however, the lands of the Celts were invaded by other peoples. First came the Romans, who were building a massive empire that covered western and central Europe. Hundreds of years later, many new tribes, including the Angles and Saxons, forced the Celts from their homes and took over their lands.

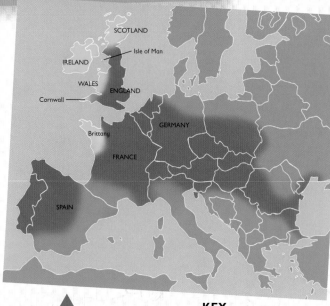

The Celts spread out across Europe and still live in the UK and France today.

KEY

▮ Celtic lands in the 3rd century BC
▮ Modern Celtic nations

MAKE A CARNYX BROOCH

A carnyx was a trumpet in the shape of a boar's head, which was blown by the Celts in battle.

◀ This is a modern copy of an ancient Celtic carnyx found in Scotland. It has a movable tongue and lower jaw.

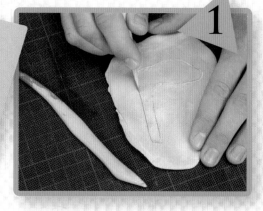

1

On a flat sheet of modeling clay, sketch the outline of the carnyx. It should be about 4 in (10 cm) by 4 in (10 cm).

4

When the clay is dry, paint the carnyx's body brown, its tongue red, and its eye yellow and red.

4

CELTS TODAY

Celtic culture still exists in parts of Europe. In Ireland, Scotland, Wales, and northern France, versions of the Celtic language are still used. The Celtic culture also lives on in the **literature**, music, and songs of these countries. Enya, for example, is a popular Irish singer who performs Celtic music with a modern twist.

THE IRON AGE

The first Celts lived during a period called the Iron Age, which lasted from about 1000 BC to AD 400. This was the time when people began using iron to make **weapons** and **tools**. They also made things from bronze, including the carnyx—a battle trumpet.

Celts were skilled metalworkers. Weapons such as this dagger handle were often made from bronze.

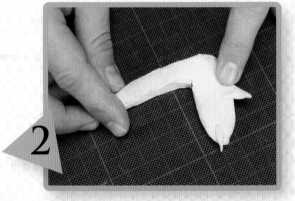

2 Cut out the brooch shape. Make the ears and tongue from separate pieces of clay and stick them on.

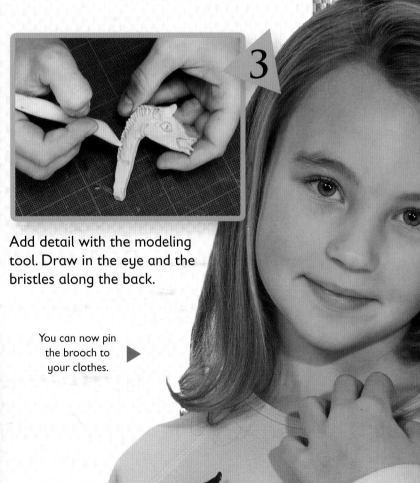

3 Add detail with the modeling tool. Draw in the eye and the bristles along the back.

5 Once the paint is dry, stick a safety pin on the back with sticky tape.

You can now pin the brooch to your clothes. ▶

5

TRIBAL LIFE

Unlike the Romans, the Celts did not belong to a single empire ruled by one leader. Instead, they lived in groups called tribes. Each tribe lived alone and was separate from the other tribes. However, the Celts all shared a similar culture and spoke versions of the same language. Tribes did not usually live in one place, but often moved around in search of food. Sometimes, tribes would fight each other over land.

▲ The Celts were skilled horsemen. They used horses to find new territory, as well as in battle.

THE LEADER OF THE TRIBE

A Celtic tribe had several **hierarchy** levels. At the top was the chieftain, who was in charge. Below the chieftain were the warriors, who protected the tribe, and the Druids, who were responsible for religious ceremonies. Next came the farmers, who provided the food, while at the bottom were the slaves.

◄ Vercingetorix was the leader of the Arverni tribe in Gaul, modern-day France. He was defeated by the Roman leader Julius Caesar.

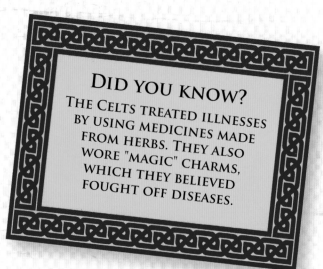

DID YOU KNOW?

THE CELTS TREATED ILLNESSES BY USING MEDICINES MADE FROM HERBS. THEY ALSO WORE "MAGIC" CHARMS, WHICH THEY BELIEVED FOUGHT OFF DISEASES.

CELTIC TALL TALES

The ancient Celts did not have a written language, so much of what we know about them comes from Roman writers. However, we cannot be sure that the Romans always told the truth. The Celts were their enemies and the Roman writers sometimes exaggerated their stories.

Celtic coins often had animal designs on them.

MAKE CELTIC COINS

Many Celtic tribes created their own coins from silver, bronze, or gold. Each tribe had its own design, such as a horse or warrior.

YOU WILL NEED
NON-DRYING CLAY
MODELING TOOL • PLASTER OF
PARIS • GOLD OR SILVER PAINT •
PAINTBRUSH • WATER
PAIR OF COMPASSES • PENCIL

1 Draw a 1.5-in (4-cm) circle onto the clay. Scoop out the circle to a 0.1 in (3 mm) depth. This is the coin mold.

2 With the modeling tool, draw a Celtic design into the coin mold. Make the design fairly deep.

3 Mix the plaster of Paris with water. Pour the mixture into your coin mold until it's completely full.

4 When the plaster is dry, peel away the clay to reveal your coin.

Paint your coin a bright gold or silver color. Start again and make more coins.

Try different designs on your coins. Horses were often featured on Iron Age Celtic coins.

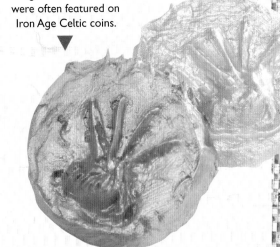

5

Under Roman Rule

The Romans could not conquer the Celtic tribes in northern Britain, so they built Hadrian's Wall to stop them invading the south.

From the 1st century BC onward, the Romans built an empire that stretched across Europe. They fought many battles with the Celts and took over many of their lands. The Romans didn't always drive the Celts out of their homes. They would often allow the Celts to continue living where they were, so long as they accepted the Romans as their new rulers.

CELTS AND ROMANS TOGETHER

Once the battles were over, and the Romans and Celts started to live together, they became more friendly. Some Celts began to copy the culture of the Romans. They dressed in Roman dress and joined in Roman practices, such as bathing in public baths and speaking in Latin—the Roman language. Some Celts even married Romans or joined the Roman army.

DID YOU KNOW?

After victory in battle, the Romans would take a few Celts away as slaves. Most, however, would be allowed to return home. Some Celtic tribes also kept slaves.

FORCING OUT THE CELTS

When the Roman Empire ended in the 5th century AD, new tribes began to move across Europe looking for land. The Angle and Saxon tribes decided to invade Britain. However, unlike the Romans, they were not willing to share and forced the Celts out. They took over much of what is now England, pushing the Celts west into Wales and Cornwall.

Celtic warriors sometimes fought on horseback or using small chariots.

MAKE A
CELTIC CHARIOT

Although most Celts fought on foot, some very important warriors would charge into battle using horse-drawn chariots.

YOU WILL NEED
CARDBOARD CEREAL BOX
THICK CARDSTOCK • PAIR OF
COMPASSES • SCISSORS
GLUE • PENCIL • PAINTBRUSH
AND PAINT • DRAWING PINS
RULER • MARKER PEN

1

Cut out a section from a cereal box, 4 in (10 cm) high and 3 in (8 cm) wide. This will be the chariot carriage.

2

Draw two half circles, 3 in (8 cm) in diameter, either side of the chariot carriage. Carefully cut them out.

3

Cut out a T-shape, 3 in (8 cm) wide and 1 in (2 cm) long from the long side of the box. This is the **yoke**.

4

For the wheels, draw two circles on a piece of cardstock, each 2.7 in (7 cm) in diameter. Cut them out. Paint the pieces.

5

Cut the thick cardstock the same width as the chariot and stick it underneath with glue. Attach the wheels with pins.

A chariot was a precious object that would often be buried with its owner. ▶

Fearsome Warriors

Warriors were an important part of Celtic society. The Celts often had to fight, either to take over new land, or to defend themselves against their enemies. The men would train to fight from a young age. Before a battle, the warriors would make themselves look scary by covering their bodies and faces in bright-blue paint, known as wood, and by spiking up their hair using **lime**.

The Celts fought fiercely, but were usually beaten by the Romans.

Make the Dye for a Celtic Warrior's Battle Paint

The Celts used dyes from plants and berries to paint scary patterns on their faces before going into battle.

With their blue face paint and loud war cries, the Celts were terrifying opponents in battle.

YOU WILL NEED
RED CABBAGE • 1 LEMON
WATER • 2 JARS • CARDSTOCK
STRAINER • PENCIL • KNIFE
CUTTING BOARD
PAINTBRUSH AND PAINTS

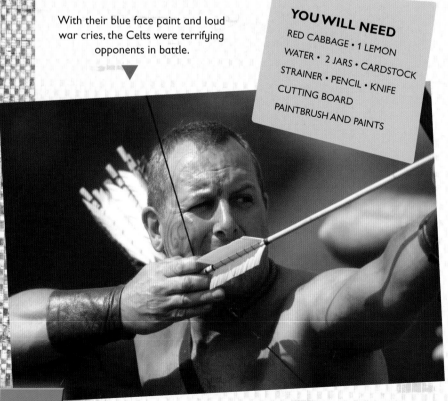

First, draw a picture of a Celtic warrior's face. The warrior can be a man or a woman.

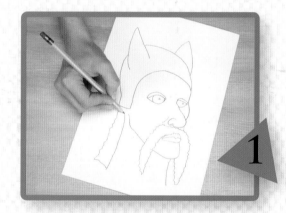

Remove the cabbage by straining the purple mixture through a strainer into the other jar.

10

WARRIOR WOMEN

It wasn't just men who fought in Celtic society. One of the most famous Celtic warriors of all time was a woman called Boudicca. She was the chief of the Iceni tribe in Britain, and led a **revolt** against the Romans in AD 60. She rode at the head of her army in a horse-drawn chariot. Roman writers said she had long, red hair.

Boudicca, a British Celtic chieftain, destroyed three British towns, before she was defeated.

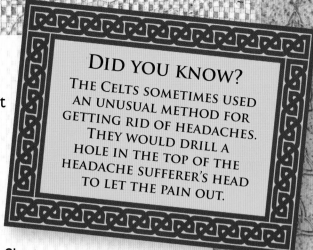
BATTLE CRIES

The Celts did not fight in an organized way—instead they surprised their enemies, attacking them suddenly and without warning. They also blew loud war trumpets and shouted at their enemies.

To make the dye, ask an adult to slice half a red cabbage into small strips and place it in a jar.

Squeeze the juice of a whole lemon onto the cabbage. Cover with cold water and leave to stand for an hour.

Use the cabbage dye and paint to add fearsome patterns on your Celtic warrior's face.

War paint was meant to frighten the Celts' enemies, so make your warrior look scary.

WEAPONS AND ARMOR

The Celts used a number of different weapons in battle. From far away, the Celts would throw long wooden spears topped with sharp iron points, and hurl small stones using a **sling shot**. Then, the warriors would charge at their opponents with their sharp swords and daggers made of iron. The Romans said that the Celts were so fond of fighting that they would often attack each other, if they couldn't find anyone else to fight.

This British bronze helmet dates from around 150–50 BC.

WAR HELMETS

The most important warriors would protect themselves against their enemies by wearing helmets made of bronze, iron, or leather. The insides were padded with soft cloth, while the outsides were decorated with ornate patterns. Some warriors had horns on the top of their helmets to make them look even more scary.

DID YOU KNOW?
THE CELTS USED TO FIGHT NAKED TO INTIMIDATE THEIR ENEMIES.

The Celts often made their shields very long to protect as much of their body as possible.

ARMOR AND SHIELDS

Armor was made from **chain mail** and was very expensive. Only a few warriors could afford to wear it. Every warrior, however, would carry a shield made from leather and wood. A shield was one of the Celtic warrior's most important possessions. Celtic shields would be decorated with patterns that may have had religious meanings, although we cannot be sure.

Celtic warriors carried their shields in one hand and a weapon in the other.

MAKE A CELTIC WAR HELMET

The Celts wore many different styles of helmets. Some had ear and nose guards and others had large horns.

YOU WILL NEED
BALLOON • OLD NEWSPAPER
WHITE SCHOOL GLUE
SCISSORS • THIN CARDSTOCK
PAINTBRUSH AND BRONZE
PAINT • GLUE • PIN

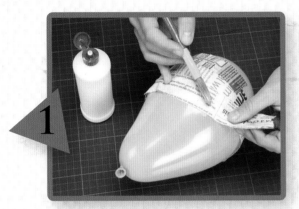

1

Blow up the balloon to the size of your head. Apply strips of newspaper covered with glue to the top half.

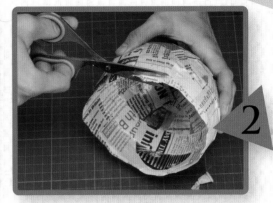

2

When dry, pop the balloon and remove it. Trim away any jagged edges. Paint the helmet bronze.

3

Cut out two triangles, 12 in (30 cm) by 8 in (20 cm). Fold into cone shapes and stick together with glue.

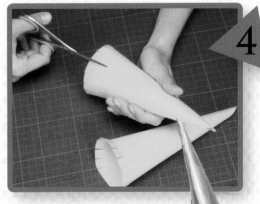

4

Make 0.5 in (1 cm) long cuts, around the horns all the way round.

5

Press out the cuts, cover with glue and attach to your helmet. Paint the horns bronze.

When dry, you could decorate your helmet with symbols and patterns—just like the Celts did. ▶

13

FORTS AND HOUSES

Most Celts lived peaceful lives in small villages near their farms. The Celts also often built defended settlements, called hill forts, for times of conflict. They surrounded these forts with tall earth walls and deep ditches to keep out attackers. Built up high, the forts would give a good view of approaching enemies, allowing the people to retreat inside the fort's walls before the attackers arrived.

▲ The ditches surrounding the Celtic hillfort of Maiden Castle in England made it difficult to attack.

MAKE A ROUNDHOUSE

Celtic families often lived in simple round homes, called roundhouses, with mud walls and straw roofs. A roundhouse could be up to 50 ft (15 m) across.

YOU WILL NEED

THIN CARDSTOCK • RULER
PAINTBRUSH AND PAINTS • GLUE
SCISSORS • PAIR OF COMPASSES
STRIP OF CORRUGATED
CARDBOARD • DRY SPAGHETTI
GREEN CARDSTOCK • PENCIL

1

Cut out a 12 in (30 cm) by 2 in (5 cm) piece of cardstock. In the center, draw a door and cut out. Paint one side yellow.

▲ Iron Age Celtic roundhouses had one door, but no windows, as this modern reconstruction shows.

4

Cut a line from the circle's center to the edge. Fold around to make a cone shape and glue together.

5

Stick on dry spaghetti to make it look like straw. Place the roof on top of the wall. Paint the roof yellow.

14

INSIDE A CELTIC HOUSE

There was very little furniture inside a roundhouse. The family slept on an earth platform that was covered with straw and they would wrap themselves in furs to keep warm. Meals would be eaten sitting on the floor or at a low table. Weapons and tools would hang on the walls.

◀ The roundhouse roof was supported by a frame of wooden poles.

THE FIRE

Celtic life revolved around the roundhouse fire. The smoke escaped through gaps in the straw roof, so the house must have been smoky inside. The fire provided heat and was used to cook the daily meals.

2

When dry, glue the ends together. The ends should overlap. This is the wall.

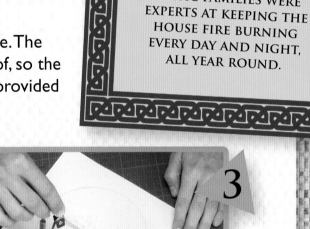

3

Mark out a circle for the roof, 6 in (15 cm) in diameter on another piece of cardstock. Cut it out.

Put your roundhouse and fence on some green cardstock to show the land.

▼

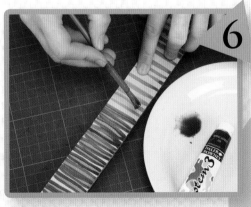

6

Paint the corrugated cardboard brown with wooden posts. Place around your roundhouse.

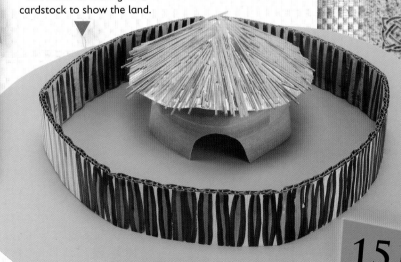

EVERYDAY LIFE

When they weren't fighting—which didn't happen that often—the Celts' main job was farming. Celts would usually try to build their settlements near fertile soils and fresh water. Celtic farmers planted crops such as wheat for making bread. They also kept animals, including pigs, cattle, sheep, and goats, which provided meat, milk, leather, furs, and wool. The animals' **manure** would be used to fertilize the fields.

The Celts ground corn between two stones, known as quern stones, to get flour.

DID YOU KNOW?
THE CELTS DID NOT HAVE MODERN REFRIGERATORS. IF THEY WANTED TO SAVE A PIECE OF MEAT OR FISH, THEY WOULD COVER IT IN SALT TO MAKE IT LAST LONGER.

CELTIC CLOTHES

The Celts made clothes from wool, which they colored using dyes from plants and berries. It is thought they liked clothes made of bright, checked patterns, a bit like the modern tartans worn by people in Scotland. Women wore dresses, which they held together using **brooches**. Men wore tunics and trousers, which they held up with a leather belt. Both men and women wore leather shoes.

FOOD AND DRINK

The people of the tribe ate the food they grew in the fields and their farm animals. However, they also picked wild fruit, berries, and mushrooms, and hunted and fished in local woods and rivers. Most of their food was cooked over the fire.

This is a recreation of a Celtic chieftain's roundhouse in Wales, built on the site of the original house.

Firedogs were used to raise the logs of the fire off the floor.

MAKE A FIREDOG

Firedogs were ornate metal stands that the Celts put next to the fire to symbolize its great importance.

YOU WILL NEED
CARDSTOCK • CARDBOARD TUBE • PENCIL • PAINTBRUSH AND PAINTS • SCISSORS

Take a piece of cardstock, about 12 in (30 cm) by 8 in (20 cm) and fold it in two along its width.

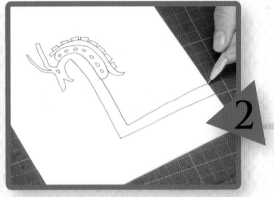

On one half of the cardstock, sketch half of the firedog shape, right up to the fold.

Carefully cut around the firedog, through the folded cardstock. Paint and decorate both sides.

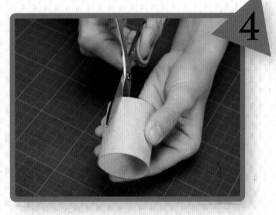

Cut the cardboard tube in half to make the stands. Cut a slot about 1 in (2.5 cm) long in the top of each stand.

Paint the stands and leave them to dry. Slide your firedog into the stands.

Make sure you don't put your firedog anywhere near a fire.

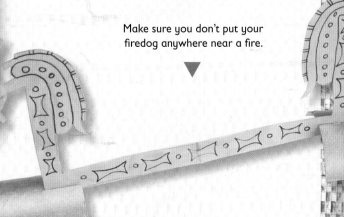

17

ARTS AND CRAFTS

The Celts used their amazing metalworking skills to create beautiful, intricate pieces of jewelry, which were worn by both men and women. They also made pots from clay, and beads and bracelets from glass. These items were not only supposed to look good, they also showed how important the owner was. The most powerful members of the tribe would have objects made from the most precious materials.

This helmet is decorated in the La Tène art style, which used complicated patterns and shapes.

DID YOU KNOW?

BETWEEN AROUND 100 BC AND AD 500, THE CELTS DEVELOPED A VERY DISTINCTIVE STYLE OF ART, KNOWN AS LA TENE, AFTER A PLACE IN SWITZERLAND WHERE LOTS OF CELTIC OBJECTS HAVE BEEN FOUND.

CLUES FROM THE PAST

Many of the things made by the ancient Celts disappeared long ago. Soft materials, such as wood used for housing, and leather and wool used for clothes, quickly rot away. However, metal, clay, and glass objects last for a very long time. These items have provided us with important clues about the way the Celts lived.

Celts checked their appearance in polished bronze mirrors.

METALWORK

Metal, for making weapons and tools, was extremely important to the Celts. It took a long time to become a skilled metalworker. There were several stages to complete, including putting the liquid metal into molds and hammering it into the right shape.

18

MAKE A TORC

Important warriors would wear thick necklaces, called torcs, in battle. They were made of iron, bronze, or gold.

YOU WILL NEED
MODELING CLAY
PAINTBRUSH AND SILVER, GOLD OR BRONZE PAINTS

The Celts believed that torcs had magical powers, which would protect them.

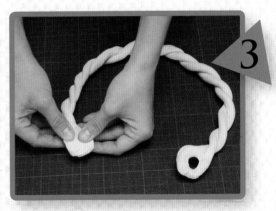

Roll out two thin lengths of modeling clay, about 24 in (60 cm) long. Don't make them too thin.

Twist them together, so they look like braided hair. Curl the torc into a loose loop.

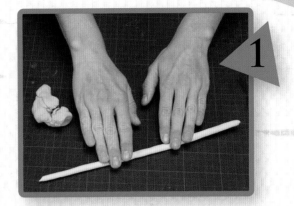

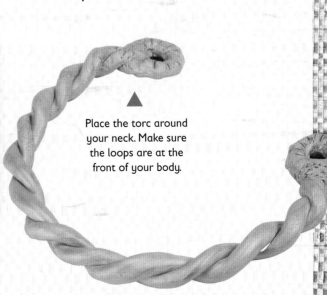

At each end of the torc, push the two loose ends together to form a small loop.

When dry, paint the torc with gold, silver, or bronze paint.

Place the torc around your neck. Make sure the loops are at the front of your body.

DRUIDS AND RELIGION

The ancient Celts worshipped many different gods, who they believed controlled the world's natural forces—such as the Sun, the Moon, and the wind. The Celts also prayed to their gods for victory in battle. Sometimes, when a Celt died, they would be buried wearing their best clothes and with their favorite weapons and jewelry. The Celts thought the dead traveled to a land of spirits, where they would be able to use these items again.

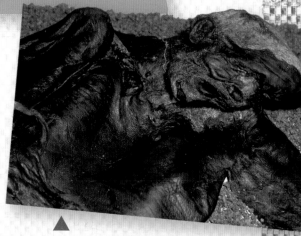

▲ These are the remains of a Celtic man who was killed about 2,000 years ago.

SACRIFICE

Celts tried to keep their gods happy through sacrifice—by giving something precious to the gods. This could be an object, such as a weapon, which they might toss into a lake where they believed the god lived. A sacrifice was often an animal, which would be slaughtered in a sacred place. Sometimes, the Celts would even sacrifice humans.

This picture shows druids cutting mistletoe, a sacred plant to them.
▼

DID YOU KNOW?
CELTS BELIEVED IN REINCARNATION. THEY THOUGHT THAT AFTER DEATH, A PERSON WOULD BE RE-BORN AS AN ANIMAL OR EVEN ANOTHER PERSON.

◄ Celts used their daggers in battle when fighting at close quarters.

DRUIDS

Druids were responsible for the Celts' religious ceremonies. Druids were usually the oldest and wisest members of the tribe, as it took many years to learn all the ancient **rituals**—perhaps as long as 20 years. Druids would make many important decisions, such as when to go to war and what happened to people who committed crimes.

MAKE A CELTIC DAGGER AND SCABBARD

Celtic daggers were very precious objects and would only be offered to the gods on important occasions.

YOU WILL NEED
CARDSTOCK • PENCIL
PAINTBRUSH AND PAINTS
SCISSORS • ALUMINUM FOIL
STICKY TAPE

1 Cut the dagger handle 3 in (8 cm) and the blade 5 in (12 cm). Cover the blade in foil. Paint the handle.

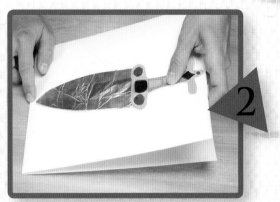

2 Fold a piece of cardstock in two. Place the dagger on one side with the blade 0.5 in (1 cm) from the fold.

3 Trace around the blade. Add a circle at the bottom and two semicircular tabs—one either side.

4 Cut around the scabbard, through the folded cardstock. Cut around the tabs.

5 Fold the two sides together. Now fold over the front tabs and stick them down. Paint your scabbard.

▶ Wealthy Celts had their scabbards plated with gold.

21

FESTIVALS AND FEASTS

Celtic feasts would often go on all day and all night.

The Celts divided the year into two main parts, summer and winter. The beginning of each was celebrated with a festival, including a feast, music, and storytelling. The most important festival was Samhain (say "sow-in") on October 31, which was the beginning of the Celtic year and the start of winter. At this time, spirits of the dead were thought to enter the world of the living and walk the earth. Today, this festival is called Halloween.

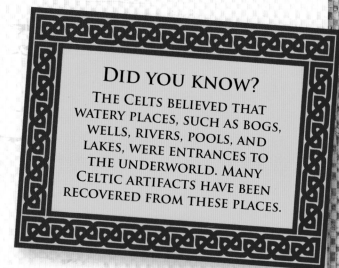

DID YOU KNOW?
THE CELTS BELIEVED THAT WATERY PLACES, SUCH AS BOGS, WELLS, RIVERS, POOLS, AND LAKES, WERE ENTRANCES TO THE UNDERWORLD. MANY CELTIC ARTIFACTS HAVE BEEN RECOVERED FROM THESE PLACES.

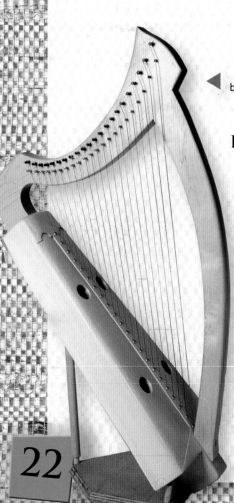

In the Middle Ages, harps became very popular in Ireland.

FEASTS
The feast was a main part of Celtic culture, when the people of the tribe would come together to enjoy a large meal. There would be lots of food, including wild boar roasted on spits, which would be eaten with bread and washed down with wine and mead.

BARDS
Bards were important members of Celtic society. It was their job to remember the **legends** and stories of the tribe and to tell them during the feast. Feasts were happy times when the tribe would come together to celebrate. They would sing and play instruments such as lyres, flutes, harps, and drums.

MAKE A CELTIC HARP

Historians believe that Celts have been using wooden harps to make music for more than 2,000 years.

YOU WILL NEED
THICK CARDSTOCK • SCISSORS
PAINTBRUSH AND SILVER PAINT
STRING • MARKER PEN • RULER
PENCIL

1 Copy the harp frame (below) onto the cardstock. The harp should be 12 in (30 cm) by 12 in (30 cm).

2 Cut out the harp frame and paint it silver. When it dries, decorate with Celtic symbols.

3 Mark 12 dots, 1 in (2 cm) apart, along the top edge of the harp. Do the same along the slanted side.

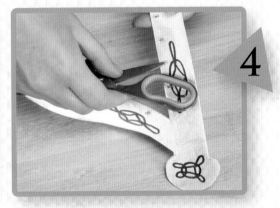

4 Get an adult to punch a small hole through each dot, using scissors.

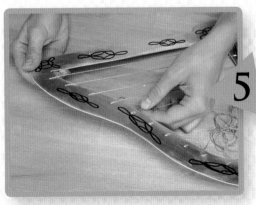

5 Attach pieces of string across the center of the harp and tie tightly in place. Cut off any loose ends.

In Iron Age times, harp strings were made from animal intestines.

23

FROM PAGANS TO CHRISTIANS

Over time, the Celts became influenced by other cultures and abandoned their own religion, which we call **paganism**. From the 1st century BC to the 5th century AD, most Celts lived within the Roman Empire. So when the Roman Empire began **converting** to Christianity in the 4th century AD, so did most of the Celts. By the time the Roman Empire ended, paganism had almost died out and most of the Celts had become Christians.

In Christian times, tall crosses marked Celtic graves.

MISSIONARIES AND SAINTS
Ireland and Scotland were never part of the Roman Empire, but the Celts who lived there were converted to Christianity by **missionaries** from Europe. St. Patrick persuaded the Irish to become Christians in the early 5th century AD, and, according to legend, also drove out all the snakes from Ireland.

This is an illustration from the Book of Kells, written by Celtic monks.

DID YOU KNOW?
KING ARTHUR, FROM BRITISH LEGEND, WAS A CHRISTIAN CELT. HE FOUGHT AGAINST THE ANGLO-SAXONS AFTER THE COLLAPSE OF THE ROMAN EMPIRE.

CHRISTIANITY IN A CELTIC STYLE
Despite becoming Christians, the Celts continued their own traditions. **Monks** in Scotland and northern England learned Latin so they could copy Christian writings, which they decorated with Celtic designs. The burial sites of Celtic Christians would also often be marked by Celtic crosses—Christian crosses decorated with Celtic patterns.

Make a Celtic Knot Bookmark

In the Christian era, the Celts developed a very original style of art using cleverly detailed patterns, known as Celtic knots.

YOU WILL NEED
TRACING PAPER • PENCIL
COLORED CARDSTOCK
PIECE OF RIBBON • HOLE
PUNCH MARKER PEN

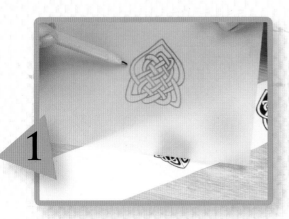

1

Carefully trace the outline of one of the Celtic knot symbols, shown at the bottom of this page.

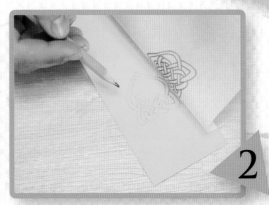

2

Transfer your tracing to the top of a piece of colored cardstock, 8 in (20 cm) by 2.5 in (6 cm).

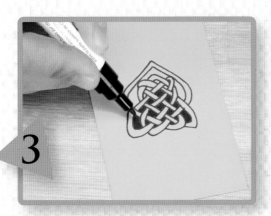

3

Color in the solid areas of the design using marker pen.

4

Punch a hole near the bottom of the cardstock. Thread your ribbon through the hole and tie it in a knot.

Make bookmarks for family and friends with different colored cardstock and designs.

CELTIC WRITING

The earliest Celts didn't have a written language, but from the 1st century AD onward, forms of writing did begin in the British Isles. In Ireland, a system of writing called Ogham was developed. It was made up of a simple system of crossed lines. This writing was read from top to bottom and left to right.

An Ogham stone used as a memorial stone.

GRAVES AND MEMORIALS

One of the main uses of Ogham was to mark names on graves, so that the Celts could remember their ancestors. The **inscription** would usually list the person's name, their father's name, and the name of their tribe.

POET'S STAFF

Bards were poets, musicians, and singers, who had to remember the Celts' history and legends. Some historians believe that bards may have carried an object called a poet's staff, on which the tribe's tales would be written down. This would have helped the bard remember all of the information.

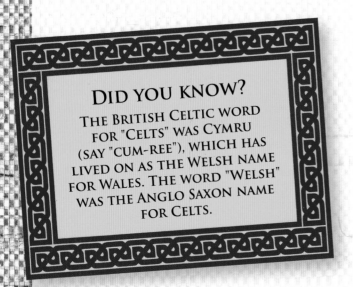

The Ogham alphabet.

MAKE AN OGHAM NAMETAG

Ogham was different from English. English has some letter sounds, such as J and W, that are not present in Ogham.

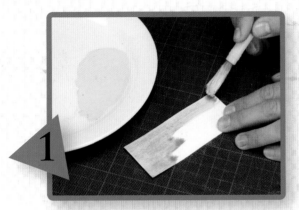

Cut out a 4 in (10 cm) by 1.5 in (4 cm) cardstock rectangle. Paint pale blue and leave to dry.

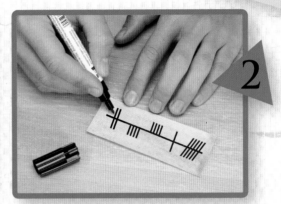

Write a name onto the cardstock, using the Ogham alphabet. Darken the lines with a marker pen.

Put a thin line of glue around the edge of the cardstock.

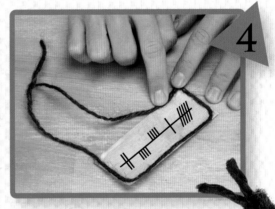

Take a long piece of green yarn and stick around the edge of the cardstock.

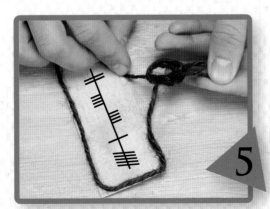

Tie the loose ends of wool together, leaving some left over so you can hang up your nametag.

You could use the string to hang your Ogham nametag from your bedroom door.

MODERN CELTS

There are several places in Europe that still have very strong Celtic cultures. These include the countries of Ireland, Scotland, Wales, the county of Cornwall in England, the province of Brittany in France, and the Isle of Man. Together, they are known as the "Six Celtic Nations". In these communities, people engage in many activities, including Celtic music, art, and dancing.

▲ Today, people in Scotland wear kilts with tartan patterns very similar to those worn by the ancient Celts.

MAKE AN IRISH STEW

Stews were an important part of the Celtic diet. Over the years, ingredients have been added, including onions and potatoes.

YOU WILL NEED
AN ADULT TO OVERSEE THE CHOPPING AND COOKING
3.3 LB (1.5 KG) OF LAMB OR CHICKEN • 4 CHOPPED POTATOES
4 CHOPPED ONIONS • 4 CHOPPED CARROTS • 17 FL OZ (500 ML) STOCK • 2 SPRIGS OF PARSLEY
SALT AND PEPPER • OIL • JUG SAUCEPAN • WOODEN SPOON

▲ Irish stew is known as "Stobhach Gaelech" in Irish Gaelic.

1

Cut the meat into small pieces and fry in a little oil until brown.

4

Simmer the stew for an hour, then add the chopped potatoes. Simmer for another hour.

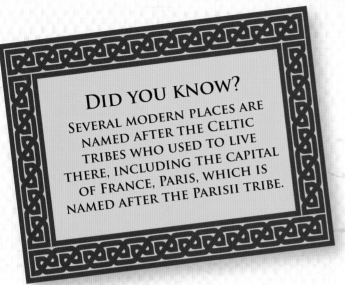
MODERN LANGUAGES

There are seven modern Celtic languages, which are all versions of ancient Celtic. These are Breton (Brittany), Cornish (Cornwall), Welsh (Wales), Irish Gaelic (Ireland), Scottish Gaelic (Scotland), and Manx (The Isle of Man). Some, such as Welsh and Irish Gaelic, are still widely spoken.

CELTIC FOOD

In Iron Age times, Celts would have made stews of meat, vegetables, and grain all cooked together in a large pot. Grains, such as wheat and barley, were the Celts' main source of food. They were picked in early fall and stored in underground pits during the winter.

Add the chopped onions and carrots and fry until soft.

Carefully add the stock, then season with salt and pepper.

Before you eat your stew, wish your friends "good health" in Irish Gaelic by saying "Sláinte" (say "slawn-che").

Add the chopped parsley, serve and eat.

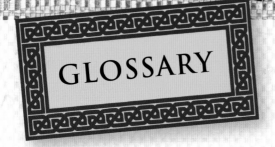

GLOSSARY

Brooch A piece of jewelry worn on the clothes and held on with a pin. Brooches can also be used to pin clothes together.

Chain mail A type of armor made up of small, interlinking chains, or rings, of metal.

Convert To get people to believe in a different religion, such as Christianity.

Dye Something that is used to change the color of something else.

Hierarchy The way people are ranked into groups in society, one above the other, according to their importance.

Inscription Words cut into a piece of stone or wood.

Legend A traditional story, usually about a hero having an adventure, that has great importance to a group of people. Legends are often made up.

Lime A white substance that contains calcium. It is made by burning limestone, bones, or shells and is spread on fields to improve the soil.

Literature Books, poems, and other forms of writing that are generally thought to be of a very high quality.

Manure The dung of animals, used to fertilize—or put nutrients into—the soil for the growing of crops.

Missionary Someone who goes to another country to try to convert the people there to a new religion, usually Christianity.

Monk Someone living in a special Christian community called a monastery.

Paganism A term used to describe the religions followed by the people of Europe before Christianity. This usually involved the worship of many gods.

Revolt A rebellion against authority.

Ritual Ceremony or way of doing something, according to particular beliefs and practices.

Sling shot A weapon that uses a long cord or piece of cloth to throw a stone with great force.

Tool An object used to do a particular job, such as a spade for digging.

Weapon Any object, such as a spear, dagger, arrow, or gun, used for fighting.

Yoke A wooden bar used for holding two animals together when they are pulling a heavy load, such as a chariot.

INDEX

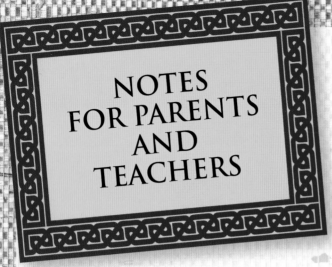

NOTES FOR PARENTS AND TEACHERS

- There are plenty of Celtic activities available at www.bbc.co.uk/wales/celts/, a website dedicated to the Iron Age Celts of Wales. You can watch cartoons on what life was like in Celtic times —or use the site's characters to create your own cartoon strip—build a virtual hillfort, design a torc, and test your knowledge of Iron Age life with a quiz.

- The Celts didn't have a written language, so much of what we know about them comes from the works of Roman writers. At http://resourcesforhistory.com you can read what the Roman writers thought of the Celts. Ask the children to write their own account of what a Celt might have thought of the Romans. At the website, you can also explore an interactive map showing how the Celts spread out across Europe, and how their lands were later taken over by the Romans, as well as read reviews of books on Celtic subjects.

- Follow a Celtic timeline from the Ice Age to the modern day, look at examples of Celtic art, and do a Celtic jigsaw at www.gallica.co.uk/celts/contents.htm. You could create a giant Celtic timeline for the classroom.

- Take online tours through the British Museum's extensive collection of original Celtic artifacts to learn about religion, war, and daily life in Iron Age Britain at www.britishmuseum.org/explore/online_tours/britain.aspx.

- Read the story of Boudicca's revolt as told from the point of view of a Roman governor, a Roman soldier, a Celtic farmer, and the Queen herself, and then answer some questions, and take a series of challenges at http://www.bgfl.org/bgfl/custom/resources_ftp/client_ftp/ks2/history/boudicca/index.htm. Ask the children to write an account of another period in Celtic history—perhaps when the Romans left Britain in the 5th century AD.

Useful websites

- See how the Celts built their roundhouses at this excellent online demonstration: http://www.bbc.co.uk/history/interactive/animations/ironage_roundhouse/index.shtml.

- Watch animations of the discovery and reconstruction of a Celtic chariot burial in Wetwang, Yorkshire, England, at http://www.bbc.co.uk/history/interactive/animations/wetwang_chariot/index.shtml.

- This site has extensive information on the world of the ancient Britons and also provides a comprehensive reading list and links to many other sites: www.gallica.co.uk/celts/contents.htm.